KENN BIVINS

39 LESSONS FOR BOYS

KENN BIVINS

39 LESSONS FOR BOYS

INVISIBLE ENNK PRESS · ATLANTA

All inquiries received at Invisible Ennk Press, P.O. Box 69, Avondale Estates, GA 30002.

First printing, 2019. Published by Invisible Ennk Press

paperback ISBN: 978-0-9853707-6-3
ebook ISBN: 978-0-9853707-7-0

Design by Kenn Bivins

for kenn and spencer

It is easier to build strong children than to repair broken men.

– Frederick Douglass

The legacy of a father is what he leaves in his stead for his children and those who have been in the shadow of his influence. I love my sons and the following are 39 lessons or snippets of wisdom I hope to teach (or have taught) them over the years.

If you have a son, nephew, mentee or boy in your life, you may benefit from this addendum to what you're already teaching. This is not a comprehensive list, but more so a foundation to build upon.

love and laugh forever,
Kenn Bivins

01

MANHOOD IS EARNED, NOT INHERITED

The biological emergence of becoming a man should not be confused with manhood. Manhood is accepting responsibility for yourself and your actions, tending to the care and well-being of others and contributing to society.

02

THERE IS A GOD...

Acknowledging that there is a being greater than yourself, creates a sense of purpose and humility that fuels endless curiosity, seeking and learning.

03

YOU ARE NOT HIM

Don't be judgemental. Instead, be humble and know that everyone makes mistakes while deserving the same grace you've been given.

04

BUT GOD DID MAKE YOU SPECIAL

The same God that made the universe
made you intentionally. No one else is like you.
That is your superpower.

05

GIVE MORE THAN YOU TAKE

Always give back to the faces and spaces that you took from.

06

DON'T RUN WITH THE CROWD, UNLESS YOU'RE THE LEADER

Lead, aspire to lead or,

while you're following,

learn to lead.

07

MAKE YOUR LIFE YOUR WORK

Find your purpose and make a living there.

08

NEVER MAKE WORK YOUR LIFE

Simply getting a paycheck is not,
and should never be all there is.

09

LOSING IS A SIGN THAT YOU'RE TRYING

Losing is only temporary. Keep trying
and learn from your losses.
You will win.

10

NEVER NEVER NEVER GIVE UP

Never.

11

NO ONE OWES YOU ANYTHING

Always be willing to work for what you want.

12

TRUE EDUCATION STARTS WHERE SCHOOL ENDS

Schooling is for the sake of demonstrating your aptitude to learn. Once you complete school, that ability is challenged and matured for the rest of your life. Therein true education ensues.

13

MONEY IS NOT EQUAL TO SUCCESS

Success is setting a goal and making it.

14

NEVER LOSE SELF-CONTROL (UNLESS YOU WANT TO)

It's called self-control because
you are in control of self.
Don't let anyone have mastery over you
that leads you to lose self-control.

15

HEALTHY RELATIONSHIPS ARE BUILT ON COMMUNICATION WHICH LEADS TO TRUST

Talking and listening build a strong rapport.

16

PHYSICAL CONFRONTATION WITH A GIRL/WOMAN = LOSE/LOSE ODDS

There is no justification for violently putting your hands on a girl or a woman.

17

CREDIT CARD DEBT IS A BRUTAL MASTER

Use credit to build wealth.

18

IF YOU CAN'T AFFORD IT WITH CASH, SAVE FOR IT OR PASS IT BY

Disciplining yourself in this way will save you from the heartache of buyer's remorse and you'll value your purchases so much more when you take the time to consider them.

19

LEARNING STARTS WITH LEAVING YOUR COMFORT ZONE

If you don't challenge yourself, you won't grow.

20

INVEST IN TEACHING OTHERS WHAT YOU LEARN

And again, give back.

21

LOVE YOURSELF BEFORE YOU EXPECT A GIRL/WOMAN TO LOVE YOU

You inform others how to love you based on how you love yourself.

22

NEVER POINT A GUN THAT YOU'RE NOT PREPARED TO SHOOT

Literally and figuratively. Don't start something that you're not willing and ready to finish.

23

SOME FIGHTS ARE BEST WON BY WALKING AWAY

Every disagreement shouldn't be addressed with physical fighting. You can win many confrontations by walking away because the best victory is living to fight another day.

24

DON'T JUDGE OTHERS JUST BECAUSE THEY ARE DIFFERENT FROM YOU

You are not God.

25

LEARN FROM THE MISTAKES OF OTHERS

Julius Caesar was wrong. Experience is not the best teacher. There can be powerful lessons yielded from experience, but there also is great wisdom gleaned from the mistakes of others.

26

SAVE MORE THAN YOU SPEND

If you heed this lesson, you will be wealthy by the time you're 40.

27

GIRLS/WOMEN THINK COMPLETELY DIFFERENT FROM YOU

Learning of her and how she communicates is essential if you want to truly know her.

28

CELEBRATE THE DIFFERENCES

We were created to be different;
therefore we should celebrate that.

29

GIVE RESPECT TO OTHERS

How you treat others informs them how to treat you.

30

LET YOUR PRESENCE COMMAND RESPECT FROM ALL

Hold your head high. You are the sun.

31

GIVE THANKS DAILY FOR WHAT YOU HAVE

A thankful heart is a humble and happy heart.

32

IT'S OKAY TO CRY

Crying is a byproduct of emotion that is a trait of being human. Don't be ashamed to feel all of your feelings.

33

SMILE MORE THAN YOU FROWN

It's easier to dwell on the negative things. Challenge yourself to smile even then. People treat you differently when you smile.

34

STAND UP STRAIGHT

Remember? You are the sun. And the sun only sets at dusk.

35

(ALMOST ALWAYS) TELL THE TRUTH

Practice living in your truth always. Know when your truth (your business) isn't for everyone to hear.

36

LOOK PEOPLE IN THE EYES WHEN YOU TALK TO THEM

Some will need to indulge the fire in your eyes, while others will starve to see the humanity there.

37

ALWAYS GET THERE EARLY

When you're early, you're less stressed, you're ready for the unexpected, you get the best seat and you're always on time.

38

ALWAYS CONSIDER THE CONSEQUENCE

And take responsibility there.

39

SEEK GOD ALWAYS

Therein you'll find your purpose.

I am the dad I always wanted. My own father was absent, but I refused to let that color the type of parent I would be to my own sons.

I will admit that more than half the time, I had no clue what I was doing, but where I was green, God, grace and gummy bears covered me.
Yes, gummy bears. Boys love gummy bears.

While I was being Dad and teaching my sons, I was learning some things too. In the next few bonus pages, I want to share those things I lovingly call **4 Lessons for Big Boys**.

BONUS 1

BE PRESENT

Any male can father a child, but it takes
a real man to **be** a father to his child.

Whether divorce, distance, finance or anything,
there is no excuse why a man shouldn't
be present for his child or children.

BONUS 2

BE KIND

"Man up" is not somethinig you say to a boy.
He's not a man. He's a boy.

While you're teaching him resilience, do not discourage him with bitter words. Encourage him in kindness with equal measure of discipline.

BONUS 3

BE A FRIEND

Our children learn about relationships from us. It's healthy for them to see us in friendships beyond family members so that they know how to be a friend.

I think someone great once said, "Be the friend you want to be."

BONUS 4

BE HUMBLE

No matter how awesome, blessed, handsome, intelligent or rich you are, be humble. Confidence is a great suit, but wear it with balance or life will remind you that you're not as ________ as you think.

It's better to be humble than to be humbled.

THE SIGNIFICANCE OF 39

You may be wondering, "What's the deal with 39? Why wasn't this book called 101 Lessons or something like that? 39 is just odd."

Well, let me explain. Years ago when I was blogging regularly, I went through what I lovingly regard as my "list phase." Lists are an amazing way to quantify accomplishments, goals, things to do, things that have been done, groceries, etc.

I ran across an internet challenge to detail random things about myself and this turned into a post entitled "99 things." This was my inaugural list, but it got so much feedback that I challenged myself further to write another list and then another, each one being a quantity divisible by 3 and ending in 9. Apparently, I was also into numeric themes.

Fun fact: June is my favorite month. It's a reflective time because so many events happen that month that are significant to me. Father's Day, being among events, prompted me to write a list from a dad's perspective. My numbering pattern had landed on 39 around the time this list was conjured and thus was born – **39 Lessons for Boys**.

Numerology indicates that 39 is associated with direction and guidance in discovering life's purpose. While I didn't know this at the time of the original writing, it's kismet how that worked out.

It's amazing to me how what seems so random can actually have meaning after all. So there you have it – the significance of 39.

A STUDY GUIDE OF 21

What are lessons without study guides, right?
The following is a bonus list of lessons that I gleaned from the internet for the sake of open discussion and interpretation with your child.

These snippets can be savored by adults too, as reminders or principles to consider. Enjoy!

1. YOU ARE BEAUTIFUL.

2. LOVE YOURSELF.

3. TALK TO GOD DAILY.

4. ASK TOO MANY QUESTIONS.

5. IT'S OKAY TO NOT HAVE ALL THE ANSWERS.

6. SOME TIMES, BABY STEPS.

7. CHOOSE LIFE EVERYDAY.

8. LIFE DOESN'T COME IN FANCY WRAPPING,
BUT IT'S STILL A GIFT.

9. DON'T DO ANYTHING YOU DON'T WANT TO DO.

10. DON'T APOLOGIZE FOR WHO YOU ARE.

11. FRAME DECISIONS WITH, "WILL THIS MATTER TOMORROW? IN FIVE YEARS?"

12. DO WHAT YOU SAY.

13. HOWEVER GOOD OR BAD THE SITUATION IS, IT WILL/ALWAYS/CHANGE.

14. DON'T RUSH IT. UNLESS YOU'RE RACING.

15. YOUR BODY ISN'T WHO YOU ARE. YOUR CHARACTER IS.

16. STOP OVERTHINKING.

17. CRYING WITH SOMEONE IS BETTER THAN HEALING ALONE.

18. NOTHING LASTS FOREVER.

19. BEFORE YOU DO GREAT THINGS, DO THE SMALL THINGS WELL.

20. GOD LOVES YOU BECAUSE OF WHO GOD IS, NOT BECAUSE OF ANYTHING THAT YOU'VE DONE OR DIDN'T DO.

21. STAY CURIOUS.

Thank you for taking the time to ponder my words. I hope you enjoyed reading them as much as I did writing. If you did, tell everyone about it and where to get it ☺

39 Lessons for Girls is also available and is a great companion to this one.

love and laugh forever,
Kenn Bivins

CPSIA information can be obtained
at www.ICGtesting.com
Printed in the USA
LVHW061606071019
633403LV00010BA/3734/P

9 780985 370763